SURVIVE.

I WOKE BEFORE I BROKE

MEGHAN DUFFIELD

IG: Souljrsmanifesto

FriesenPress

One Printers Way
Altona, MB R0G 0B0
Canada

www.friesenpress.com

ISBN
978-1-03-911495-1 (Hardcover)
978-1-03-911494-4 (Paperback)
978-1-03-911496-8 (eBook)

1. POETRY, SUBJECTS & THEMES, INSPIRATIONAL & RELIGIOU

Distributed to the trade by The Ingram Book Company

TABLE OF CONTENTS

This book was born in my home, on the Canadian Prairies. I reside on the original territory of the Ininew (Cree), Anishinaabe (Ojibway), Oji-Cree, Dene, and Dakota peoples. First Nations guided our ancestors through harsh winters, taught them how to navigate the land, shared with our ancestors their experience and knowledge. Winnipeg Manitoba is located in Treaty 1 territory, and homeland to the Métis Nation.

I honour the four directions, North, South, East, and West, and am grateful to my Helping Spirits.

I acknowledge my deep appreciation of Water and Gaia. Sun and Moon. I am forever grateful for my two-legged and four-legged friends. The finned, feathered, and the crawlers.

This book is dedicated to my fellow survivors.

I see u.

How wondrous your spirit and courage.

To my mom, who radiates positivity. To my sister, who is a warrior. To Kathy for inspiring me, always. To my daughters. My daughters, who are my legacy and my greatest teachers. I am infinitely grateful for them. Ruby, thank you for walking your path with ferocity and grace beyond your years. For fighting hard and emerging stronger and more awakened than I could have ever imagined.

To my little one, Yona Moon. She is gentle and clever, an unconqerable spirit.

It is the time of the Divine Feminine—time for us to emerge. It is our time.

As the Moon rises, we will rise.

To the women who have survived, and for those who have not...your fight was and is inspiring.

I have been blessed to know many women who have supported me throughout my journey. A community of women I am forever grateful for, and whose guidance and teachings I will share.

Thanks Dad, I am infinitely grateful for your wisdom and insight.

ASCENSION

The evolution of the mind, body, and spirit is
only possible
when you learn to elevate your frequency.
Shed your skin.

Peel away that carcass, those bones, that flesh. Get to
the *Source.*

You are the Source.
Can you not see?
You are the cosmos you adorn,
you are limitless existence.
Free
Free from the focus of the skin you're in,
the mask you wear.
Your body image expectation.
You are limitless light, and stars, and energy

Divine Feminine Power -
It can't be taken from you, because it is you.
You are awakened.

You aren't a product of your environment.

You are a product of the choices you make within
that environment.

Early on you clipped my wings.

You filled me with fear and self doubt to discourage flight.

To avoid your own embarrassment if I were to fail?

I do not fail.

I suppose you don't know that.

I will not hide as you did.

Survival is finding the strength to carry on in your weakest, most vulnerable moments.

Keeping the darkness that envelopes you at bay.

THE FIRE WITHIN

Light is ever-present.

The fire within.

As long as you breathe, you burn

and as you burn

YOU RISE.

We are the unseen.

The beaten, not broken.

The life force of our planet beats within the hearts of all women.

Refusing to be extinguished by the confines of daily life, we surge forward.

Keeping the spirit of our internal fire burning.

The Human Spirit has always been my greatest inspiration.

SURVIVE.

The free world.
Stronger, better, wiser
when touched by women.

God is creative energy.
An entity whose creation
is the foundation—
and love
is
unconditional.

Man as God is not—
feulled by lust, for power
and control.

Woman is God.

The truth. The true creator,
the creator of all life.

She is the way, the truth, and the life.
No one comes to the Father unless through her.

The focus of my mind's eye...

My Third eye.

A cosmic abyss of deranged fog and stars. Swirling and dancing—enticing me.

I find substance in this flow,

yet darkness manifests itself here.

Diminishing the warmth and glow of my Ki

until no flame remains.

Only smoke, ash, and ruin.

INTEGRATION OF
THE SHADOW SELF

Forced to conform to Life's cryptic cycle.

Forced into a co-dependant relationship of monetary
need and control.

Forced to believe in a system that fails.

Forced because we have little or no choice.

We endure.

    With pulverized hand extended,

    we face retribution for our suffering.

        Retribution

        for our own suffering.

Frustration. Fear. Anxiety. Panic.

(I'm running to catch up with myself.)

I need to catch up to her; tell her I made it. That I'm okay now.

Getting to her really wasn't that hard.

Actually, I just need to believe it's fucking possible. I need to stop detaching myself from spirit with this self-doubt.

If only I would allow it.

A web of interpretation...

I am an idealist's realist. Believing sometimes that obviousness and clarity are very different words with very different meanings.

I have learned, the suffering I once endured does not define me. I have travelled my own path.

I craft my present day.

To get here I needed to survive the painful days. Claw my way out of the deep dark holes. Journey into the scary places. Work outside my comfort zone. Learn to follow my intuition.

I needed to *Live.*

Living is to suffer.

Suffering falls at love's feet.

Love is invigorating.

Salvatio.

Darkness creeps in . . .

*I feel as though there is someone inside me trying to get out this
frustrates me and makes me sad
I feel confined, and that everything I love and yearn for seems
unattainable I feel lost and misunderstood I feel underesti-
mated and a failure I feel like I have no purpose and am a
waste of space I have no idea what my contribution could be I
feel emptyifeelusedandworthlessandbadandstupidandlonely
andhorridanddisfiguredanduglyajokeawasteoverwhelmed
scaredfearfuldisappointing pleasehelpmehearmeseemepleasetry*

Inescapable grief

a chest full of it

shallow breathing

emotional claustrophobia

the horror of the truth

inescapable truth

stillness

heaviness

unfathomable sadness

anxiety in a moment of realization.

MEGHAN DUFFIELD

With a pail of water in each hand, you choose to watch
me burn.

When I rise as ash and dust you will choke on your neglect.

And I will be free.

A SURVIVOR'S MANIFESTO

A Woman's Power, Strength, Perseverance and Hard Work are the building blocks of our fundamental core.

Our ability to give selflessly, love, and offer support speaks to our empathetic nature.

Our tolerance, understanding, and patience make us compassionate allies.

We continue to be underestimated, and yet, we are the blood that runs through your veins.

We are *Heart and Soul*, the embodiment of Love and giver of *Life*.

We lead from the shadows. Anticipating the moment you have completely underestimated us. When we step to you, you will find out who we are. What Divine Power feels like, what we are capable of.

We are the daughters of Gaia and are charged with life-force energy.

We are the gatekeepers of our own destiny.

In times of powerlessness, submission, and fear, we endure. We continue to fight and find the strength to emerge from the darkness, rising above your contempt.

Transcending our place—our role—our obligation. Transcending ourselves.

We will come out on top.

When we are at our best, you will never see us coming. Our femininity should never be confused for weakness. It is our strength—our power.

We are born of the awakened womb and experience rebirth again and again.

Our strength is your weakness.

You try to hide us when we are obviously not hidden. Try to cover us up and shield us from the world, failing when beauty seeps from us still.

You try to dominate us, bully us, beat us into submission. This only makes us stronger—fueling the fire within. You try to intimidate, patronize, demoralize us in an endlessly ruthless attempt to break us.

You attempt to enslave me, rape me, torture me, hit me, mutilate me...

As the moon rises, I will rise.

You will never defeat ME.

I am stronger than you.

I will live on, and I will live on in you. I feel as though you need to be reminded of that now. You will never break my unconquerable spirit.

Integration Station

A JOURNALING SPACE

HOPE

I was lost. I was confused, and angry. My head hurt.

Then, I received a message.

Sitting across the room from me, watching my anguish, head in hand at my dinner plate.

She texted three words.

"I love you."

She woke me.

Have you ever been woke in a moment?

A single moment can change everything.

When you find the courage to jump in with absolute certainty.

You commit then and there.

Emergent light . . .

I live in a safe place where there is no fear but for fearing fear itself.

I live in an enchanted place where the energy of the earth touches me, warms me, nurtures me.

Here I have purpose.

I live in a quiet place where my soul is at peace. I am calling in and receiving. Longing to be touched again and again by Wonder.

I live in a beautiful place, where every living, breathing, life force surrounding me is activated and charged with divine energy. I am grateful to my helping spirits, and the ignitions I have experienced which allow this energy to flow.

I live in a terrifying place where I'm the only one who can see these things. I am alone. Unable to share the experience of this transformative place.

Hope is the underpinning of survival.

but.. what if I'm not strong?
What if I'm weak and vulnerable and afraid.
    Unloved. Unnoticed..
To give and give and give without expectation is to give it up.
To die caring and giving.

Passion.. my internal fire.
My longing. Passion drives me forward — the sheer will of it..
Passion is my passion.
I am either 0 or 100 but never 0.
I am all in.. I am a beast.

Woman. Yes. Instinctively Intuitively
 Beautifully Lovingly
Driven
 Strong
 Adaptable
 Radiant

I embrace clarity, the divine. Purity. Ecstasy. Love.

MEGHAN DUFFIELD

We are born with a light that shines brightly within

Divine light shines through us around us herein

This light is special

our own and our essence

It is our *will,* our *soul,* our *courage,* our *presence.*

Meghan Duffield

I am closer than ever to living my life exactly as I choose.

You will not like it.

Inspire me

Inspire me to LIVE

Inspire feelings of joy

Inspire me to feel alive

To love

Inspire me to draw breath

Inspire my soul to ignite, creating paths of light in
the shadows

Inspire me to see when my eyes no longer offer the lens
of perspective

Inspire me to always put one foot in front of the other

Inspire me with creativity, imagination, presence, awe
and wonder

Hold me accountable.

Collective inspiration

The power of positive change

Inspire me to lead

Inspire me to follow

Inspire me to elevate this human experience.

AWAKENING

Everything you do, and everything you think and feel and say, is justified by the fact that you are strong and capable. You have experience that manifests itself as you struggle to free yourself of limitations. You must acknowledge your Shadow Self.

You are about to let go.

From this day forward you will be conscious of your internal dialogue. You will affirm every day that you are indispensable.

You will trust yourself to make decisions based on your intuition, without over-analyzing everything to death.

Just flow.

Be kind to yourself and true to your nature.

Give yourself permission to be fucking powerful. YOU MEAN EVERYTHING.

You are the main character of your story.

I choose to live in the eye of the storm

I have lived here for so long

The need to push harder

dig deeper

make an impact

stir the pot...

The uninhibited joy in that

Trust your intuition

honour your body

and honour your Self.

Stand with feet planted firmly, absorbing the earth's energy from the ground below.

She is you and you are her . . .

THERE IS NO DEFEAT IN SURVIVAL
ONLY VICTORY

ENOUGH.

I finally sat with the Wolf I'd been feeding for years.

It was time to begin my Shadow Work.

Take a good hard look at who I had become.

This is when the *real* work begins, the *hardest* work.

I sat with ego, control, fear, aggression, self-doubt, dependency, addictive personality (you name it), workaholism, pain, grief, hate, hypochondria, resentment, victim mentality, masochistic tendencies, anxiety, panic, ACCOUNTABILITY, truth.

I focused on each one. I accepted my truth, accepted who I was. Held myself accountable.

Then I figured out how to cope. How to sit with those behaviors, advance beyond them.

Calm the storm—find peace within.

I began to feed the right wolf. The good wolf.

Shadow work.

It's the fucking worst!!!

I felt like this process was going to kill me. I truly wanted to die. I was overwhelmed by feelings of helplessness, uselessness, loneliness. I felt exhausted, vulnerable and trapped. Weighed down by heaviness I could not shake. I felt isolated and alone. An inescapable weight and despair....anguish.

Anguish.

Then, as I sat with the things that did not serve me, I learned to release the power I had given them. I began to find purpose in day-to-day blessings. I practised self-compassion, growth mindset, GRATITUDE.

My own light, my own joy. My Shamanic community and family. My inspirations.

Myself.

ME

I held ceremony, after a year of hell.

I wrote down the behaviors that were destroying me. I folded them up tight, each one on an individual piece of paper.

These little pieces of folded-up paper were charged with this incredibly toxic energy; I couldn't wait to get rid of them. The following day I took that little box of poison to the park and burned each bane to ash. Away from my sacred space, away from my sit spot. Within a generic fire pit that held no significance to me.

This ceremony of healing was a personal commitment to move forward and feed the good wolf.

The wolf you feed is the wolf that wins.

(Referenced: The Cherokee legend The Tale of Two Wolves)

Integration Station

A JOURNALING SPACE

HEALING

Wounds should heal when you have (ad)dressed them.

If you wear open wounds, they require your immediate attention.

If you continue to bleed, you are suffering

If you suffer long enough, you will die

If you are dying, you aren't living

If you aren't living, you aren't activated

If you aren't activated... you aren't thriving

Heal your wounds. Stoke your internal fire.
Find inspiration.

Repeat as often as necessary.

You are a garden...

You require nourishment to grow.

Does the earth surrounding you allow your roots to run deep? Do you allow it?

Do you look to the rain as a blessing? A ritual of cleansing. A gift. Is the rain plentiful? Do you acknowledge this gift as sacred?

As you accept the blessings surrounding you, do you not grow?

The sun will always shine, the light of day will return, water will flow. The earth will always lie beneath your feet.

You are a garden. Bloom with graciousness.

Nurture yourself so that you may grow.

Turn to the sun so that you may bloom.

Plant roots deeply, so that you may awaken in the spring-time with deliberate emergence; leaving the dormancy of winter behind you.

ReBirth.

More bountiful in strength, wisdom, and beauty with each passing year.

Integration Station

A JOURNALING SPACE

SURVIVE BAD SEX

SURVIVE YOUR ENVIRONMENT

SURVIVE HOMEWORK

SURVIVE DEPRESSION

SURVIVE SOCIAL MEDIA

SURVIVE ABUSE

SURVIVE SUICIDAL THOUGHTS

SURVIVE YOUR FRIENDS

SURVIVE YOUR PARENTS

SURVIVE BAD HAIR DAYS

SURVIVE BIAS

SURVIVE SYSTEMIC RACISM

SEXISM

CHAUVINISM

AGEISM

COLONIALISM

SURVIVE TOXIC RELATIONSHIPS

SURVIVE OBLIGATION

SURVIVE THE GRIND.

SURVIVE BECAUSE YOU MATTER

SURVIVE BECAUSE YOU CHOOSE TO

SURVIVE BECAUSE YOU ARE ESSENTIAL

SURVIVE.

LOVE

Love is the energy we share and the air we breathe

An intrinsic gift to be nurtured.

Love is worth fighting for

A beacon of light in our darkest hour.

Devotion—

Love is hope.

Love beyond love . . .

My intention is to cherish every moment with you.
To stand in my truth and love you with all my heart.
The way you deserve.

Spiritually uplifting

out-of-body

cosmic connectivity

hype type shit.

Intention.

Intention is not a promise, it is born of will and practise.

Everything changes when the sun comes out.

9 781039 114944